REFLECTIONS AND SHADOWS

Saul Steinberg holding

his eight-year-old self

by the hand.

REFLECTIONS AND SHADOWS

Saul Steinberg with Aldo Buzzi

TRANSLATED FROM THE ITALIAN BY JOHN SHEPLEY

RANDOM HOUSE   NEW YORK

All rights reserved under International and Pan-American
Copyright Conventions. Published in the United States
by Random House, Inc., New York, and simultaneously
in Canada by Random House of Canada Limited, Toronto.

RANDOM HOUSE and colophon are registered trademarks
of Random House, Inc.

This work was originally published in Italian as *Riflessi e ombre* by
Adelphi Edizioni S.P.A. Milano in 2001.

All illustrations by Saul Steinberg were originally published
in *The New Yorker* and are © 2002 The Saul Steinberg
Foundation/Artists Rights Society (ARS).

Library of Congress Cataloging-in-Publication Data
Steinberg, Saul.
[Riflessi e ombre. English]
Reflections and shadows/Saul Steinberg with Aldo Buzzi; translated
from the Italian by John Shepley.
p.   cm.
Includes bibliographical references.
ISBN 0-375-50571-7
1. Steinberg, Saul.   2. Artists—United States—Biography.   I.
Title.
N6537.S7 A2 2002
741'.092—dc21   2001048696
[B]

Random House website address: www.atrandom.com

Printed in the United States of America on acid-free paper

24689753

FIRST U.S. EDITION

*Frontispiece photograph by Evelyn Hofer/*GRAZIA NERI

Book design by Barbara M. Bachman

CONTENTS

FOREWORD

"This book is the fruit of tape-recorded conversations held in my country house in Springs, East Hampton, during the summer of 1974 and the autumn of 1977, with my friend Aldo Buzzi, who later made a careful selection of all the transcriptions and arranged them in four chapters."

I proposed this note to Steinberg at his request, to introduce the book once he had agreed to its publication. I had made a first draft in Milan, and then a second, shorter one, discarding some of the less-interesting portions of the material. Steinberg read both versions and preferred that we go ahead with the second one. He also approved the title, which comes from a series of drawings published in this volume: "Shadows and Reflected Images."

But then he thought it over once more and the project was left hanging. He was a man full of doubts. Perhaps he felt that as a writer he was not up to his own level as an artist, an artist who used to say that he was a writer who drew instead of writing.

Aldo Buzzi

REFLECTIONS AND SHADOWS

CHAPTER ONE

Romania.

Artistic education.

Uncles and aunts.

A family photograph.

I DIDN'T STAY LONG ENOUGH TO ENJOY THE "GOOD life" in Romania, as a man of thirty, forty, or fifty— a successful man. There were no special pastimes for young people. I had no rights, and went to high school wearing a name plate with a number, like an automobile. And above all, as long as you had no money, you couldn't enjoy the dreadful freedoms of Romania, which were invariably abuses, or lead the life of a gentleman, the sort of man who, if he has money, can always find people to buy. My childhood, my adolescence in Romania were a little like being a black in the state of Mississippi.

———

There were girls who came down from the mountains to work as servants, and they were treated like savages from the jungle, like slaves; they had almost no rights and immediately became the prey of the masters and sons of the house, of the neighbors. They came from villages as yet untouched by civilization, villages of Tatars and Visigoths, and they arrived in the confusion of a city full of every kind of scoundrel; they were flesh for the whorehouses, and often committed suicide, even for absurd reasons, such as having been unfairly scolded by their mistress or accused of stealing. They doused themselves with kerosene and lit a match.

There was plenty of kerosene, which was used in oil lamps. Peddlers went along the street with two drums of oil, yelling, "*Gase, gase.*" Women who kept company with a *gasàr* always smelled of kerosene, and this made other men avoid them.

Every so often certain smells that I haven't smelled since I was a child come back to me—not to my nose, like an actual smell, but to the nose's brain. Vague smells, and at the same time specific ones: the smell of autumn; of certain stores; the smell of early winter, when the weather starts to get cold: the first fire in the house, with the lamp lit at five in the afternoon. The metal stove had a special smell when lit for the first time, since the surface had been greased to keep it from rusting. And there was the smell of the oil lamp.

I like smelling that odor again, but it can't be called up at will. Still, it sometimes happens that all of a sudden, for some mysterious reason, the memory of that smell comes back to me.

Nothing that has been deposited in the memory is lost. Memory is a computer that all one's life goes on accumulating data which are not always used, since man is often like an ocean liner that sets sail with only a single cabin occupied. We ought to be able to use this huge accumulation of data continually, keep it functioning, combine and multiply its elements and reintroduce them into the circuit of our thoughts. So it happens with the return of these smells, deposited many years ago in the memory and now revived. Maybe I'll have the good fortune to find again other things that now seem forgotten. I'd like to be able to go back and see all the things that at the time I stored away without perceiving them, follow myself at the age of ten and judge, with the mind of today, the conditions under which I lived, thus discovering what, at that time, had been deposited in the computer without my knowing it.

I'm very much interested in the time just before my birth, and I'm sorry not to have seen it. I have the feeling that by making a mental effort I might be able to see it. It's a time so close to me that I feel as though I know it quite well, and I'm moved whenever I think of it. Maybe it's because my parents were young and didn't know each other.

grew up without toys. My father was a bookbinder; later he set up a small factory for cardboard boxes, with lots of colored paper and a great supply of glue. The factory had the smell of an artist's studio, of collages, as

well as the smell of the ink used on large wooden letters
to print the ribbons of funeral wreaths. The female
employees worked skillfully and with manual dexterity
to assemble and glue boxes of various sizes, some of
them tiny—even lipstick holders (plastic hadn't yet been
invented), little cardboard cylinders that could be
opened and closed and which were covered with colored
paper and trimmed with gold and silver. Women and
girls of all ages and sizes worked amid much laughter
and constant chatter. On Saturday, payday, a group of
men waited for them outside the factory: the boyfriends
or perhaps the pimps of the older girls, and the fathers
of the little ones, who took the money and immediately
rushed off to get drunk.

The busiest time was at Passover, when my father
managed to obtain major orders for boxes to hold
unleavened bread. Before being sent to the bakeries—
where the unleavened bread was made under rabbin-
ical supervision—these boxes, which were rather large,
were stacked up in big piles that took on the appearance
of fantastic cardboard buildings. The factory also

"Nowadays I draw uncles and aunts from photographs and I
recognize (looking at them for the first time as real people)
parts of myself, an ear, an eye. Archaeology!" (From a letter
of September 18, 1978.) The man in military uniform is
Steinberg's father, during World War I; the one in tails and
top hat, in the last drawing, is the croupier uncle.

produced boxes for chocolates, bonbons, and sugar-coated almonds—deluxe boxes on whose glossy covers was an artistic reproduction in chromolithography, the imitation or reproduction of an oil painting.

At home we had large sets of reproductions of the most popular works of art, from the Renaissance to the modern art of that time. Certain Madonnas by minor Renaissance painters managed to give a perfect image of popular Christianity, or rather of a kind of pastry cook's Christianity, what the French call *bondieuserie.* Millet was ideal for chocolate boxes because he combined the classicism of the Renaissance with socialism, which at that time was not only popular but also virginal (no one yet knew of the horrors that might come, and did come). And then there was Raphael: the Dresden Madonna; and the thinking angel, with his elbow propped on a cloud. Many of these images I was seeing for the first time, without knowing they were art, painting. Later, I ran across them again in art books and recognized them.

Another teacher, for me, was the family album. There were the pictures of relatives—uncles and aunts, cousins, grandparents, great-grandparents—from the earliest ones, taken by excellent photographers still inspired by the paintings of Delacroix and Ingres, down to the first attempts at family photos that we did ourselves, horrible photos in which everyone had a Hitler-like mustache, produced by the shadow of the nose.

These photographs were my first models. Even today I'm captivated when I see a person who, by suddenly freezing into immobility, seems like a photograph of himself and takes on a folk-art look. Photography has had a continuing effect on art. A painter such as Bacon clearly derives from the Polaroid, but at the same time it's also true that art precedes technique, just as the smell precedes the cake. Bucharest, in the days of my youth, was a peculiar city, an *enfant-prodige* city, where the avant-garde cohabited with primitivism, as in certain places where two or three rivers converge and mingle, where there is something essential that has nothing to do with the ordinary character of the place, something that emerges at a particular moment when cultures, the forces of south, north, east, and west come together and give birth to a tornado, a typhoon, a waterspout, or if you like, an eddy—Dada.

Of my many uncles, actual ones or not, two were sign painters, and for me they were the most interesting because they dealt with things that involved painting. My Uncle Moritz limited himself to painting large inscriptions on canvas mounted on frames or on canvas banners to be strung above the street on the occasion of sales, festivals, political rallies—cheap stuff, for stores that wouldn't last longer than the canvas sign. Other signs were painted directly on the wall. For these jobs my uncle sent one of his employees; it was beneath his dignity to go in person and paint a sign on a wall, which was a mark of poverty besides. Signs painted in color on glass windows were another matter. That required a specialist, and it was my uncle himself who went to do the job. He painted the letters from the inside, in reverse.

Uncle Moritz's brother Josef not only did the letters but also painted the subject. The shopkeepers thought

it over for months before hitting on the right idea for
their store signs: the golden cannon, or the sea eagle
with a fish in its claws, images intended to help the
illiterate peasants. Here, too, as in everything else in
Romania at that time, one felt the influence of Paris,
where the signs for bakeries, dairies, and pastry shops
had to have, almost always on a black background, pictures in addition to letters: oval landscapes, a shep-
herdess, scenes of happiness and nobility, artistic
stereotypes that were very important to me then, and
still are. (The Russians, so as not to whet people's
appetites, have reduced their store signs to a minimum.
If it's really necessary to show that a store sells shoes,
they barely sketch the outline of a shoe, and the rest is
written, in a tiny space.)

On mirrors or plate glass, in gold on a black background, my Uncle Josef painted a Romania that tried to
resemble the court of Versailles, with happy views of
peasants in national costume, all highly suited to pastry
shops, restaurants, and other such places. Miniaturist
craftsmen worked with small brushes in his studio, a
setting saturated with the pungent odor of turpentine.

(Much of Magritte derives from sign painting, especially when he has to depict a human figure. The whole Surrealist school tries to show man as a cliché, the standard figure copied on signs from the fashion journals of the day.)

Uncle Moritz worked outdoors, in one of those huge courtyards inside a block of houses that are found in all Balkan countries. Carpenters, cobblers, and mattress makers worked there, any artisan who needed space; there were many cafés, of course, and a restaurant, the latter busy only in the evening. Tables were scattered more or less everywhere, acres of chairs and little tables between which waiters passed quickly with large trays; also sellers of sweets, with baskets on their heads or on their arms, peddlers of dirty postcards, cheap books, stamps, newspapers; and gypsies who either read palms or were tinkers or thieves. In the middle of it all was Uncle Moritz, rapidly painting his signs, with a big stick to keep his hand steady. A crowd of children and grownups constantly gathered to watch him work.

Two of my uncles had shops where they sold stationery and books, mostly school texts and popular works: adventure stories with bandits; the story of Olympias, mother of Alexander the Great, with the horse Bucephalus; and the *Thousand and One Nights*, with those Oriental women wearing nothing but a few veils. But most of their business was in school materials: pencils, erasers, and ink—purple and blue, both of which made indelible spots on your hands, got under your fingernails, and stayed there all year. And ink pots guaranteed not to tip over, sponges for slates, notebooks with ruled pages for penmanship or graph paper for mathematics, blue paper to cover books, labels on which to write your name, surname, class, and the name of your school. At Christmastime, glass tree ornaments arrived from Germany, marvelous, brightly colored metal toys from Nuremberg, and I was sent to the store to help my uncle, partly to sell, partly to keep an eye on the customers, almost all of them thieves.

Two other uncles had started out as watchmakers, then little by little had expanded their business. One had also become a jeweler. There was an odor in his store that I can still smell with pleasure when—as seldom happens now—I pass by a watchmaker's: the odor of watchmaker's oil. My uncle worked with a magnifying lens in his eye, putting all these tiny pieces in place with his tweezers. He didn't much like for me to stand there watching. I had to be careful not to get too close and to hold my breath—otherwise the little springs flew off.

The other uncle had combined his watches with musical instruments, as well as gramophones, phonograph records, and various other merchandise. In his shop window was an automaton: a clown that moved its head and eyes and lured the peasants arriving from the country and the mountains at the central railway station nearby. The neighborhood was full of whores, poor peasant women still in shabby dresses, almost all of them barefoot. They lived in squalid tenements with balconies, precursors of the motels here, which have also become whorehouses. A latrine in common for everyone, bucketfuls of water that rained down from on high without warning, constant shouting, quarreling, brawls. At home this same uncle kept a large collection of kitsch objects: shiny drawings on glass of half-naked women, very vulgar—who knows where he found them.

My last uncle's profession was not especially important, but it was wonderful to watch him at it: he was a croupier. He spoke French and worked in the Royal Casino in Sinaia. We once went to see him, and he got us in for free.

My mother had five sisters. The eldest, the most beautiful and most admired, was Sofi, who had married Moritz Grinberg, the sign painter.

My mother, Rosa, was the second sister. Her husband was also named Moritz. To distinguish the two Moritzes, one was called Sofi's Moritz, *Moritz a lu Sofi*, and the other, my father, was *Moritz a lu Rosa*.

Then came Aneta, the wife of the croupier, Micu Cohen. *Micu* means "little." No one knew what his real name was. He was one of those men who are always called by a nickname, lucky men pampered even by people who don't know them. I, on the other hand, ever since I was a child have had a solemn name: Saul. It would have been undignified to apply the diminutive, Saulica, to the name of the king of the Israelites.

The next was Pesa. Her husband, Jack Kramer, owned the store for watches and musical instruments, and the automaton. There was another uncle, Jacques, whose name was actually Isac Jacobson and who had changed his name when he got married for the second time. He was my mother's brother, feared and adored by the six sisters as the oldest, the richest, and the most distinguished. (Another brother was far away, in America, and still another had died young, perhaps a suicide.) Uncle Isac had a fine house with servants, and in the summer went to Baden-Baden and Marienbad. As a child I had to kiss his hand and address him by the formal "you."

The fifth was Sali, who had married the bookseller Simon Marcovic. "Sali" is an imitation of the American "Sally." Maybe her real name was Sarah.

Finally the youngest of the sisters, Ana, the least good-looking and also the least esteemed. She had married Uncle Adolf, the other bookseller, a fat, lame man.

Of the six sisters, the only one still alive is Aunt Sali, who lives in Jerusalem.

———

It was a society with no mysteries. Life went on in those big courtyards, where the doors were always open and anyone could look in the windows. Children came by with chickens and ducks. The hen was in the same family as the dog and the cat, a true domestic animal, while it was outrageous to have a duck in the kitchen. The goose came in with no fuss—it had authority. Chickens walked in with dancers' steps, or at times a military gait.

I have in front of me a family photograph, taken in 1924 in Solca, a small vacation resort in the mountains of Bukovina. Primitive places, of great beauty: fir trees and rushing rivers with floating rafts made of timber being transported. The raftsmen had the reputation of outlaws—they were timber cowboys, in a way, who drove herds of tree trunks through dangerous rapids, all the way to the lumberyards. There was good air and absolute silence. The inhabitants were mountain Romanians, untouched by invasions or military occupation, who for centuries had remained completely outside the world. Alongside them lived Sephardic Jews, who believed that by the joy of poetry and with the help of wine they could arrive at faith. And there were the gypsies: music, dancing, good wine.

The girl standing at the door of the hotel is an American cousin, who was then fourteen years old and had come to Romania to visit us. In the doorway is Uncle Jean, my father's brother. A traveler has either arrived or is about to depart: there's his suitcase. His hat on his head, he is seated comfortably at the table with a companion, examining two bottles of wine. A high school pupil, in school uniform, is leaning on the door as though against a column. Two show windows display bottles of local sparkling white wine. The cook can be seen like a ghost through the third window, and on the veranda beyond are some vacationers, guests of the hotel, which was owned by a Jewish peasant.

The cooking was Jewish, partly Polish-Russian, partly northern Romanian, Hungarian, Austro-Hungarian: paprika, vegetables. On Saturday a special meal was served that had been prepared on Friday and then placed under embers to keep it warm. When it came time to eat it on Saturday, it had turned into a kind of gelatin that bore no resemblance either to the original chicken or to anything else.

There are mysterious areas in this photo. There's a man who can barely be seen—it looks like he's wearing a top hat. For a long time I didn't notice him, and I don't really know what he's doing there: an invisible man who popped out only in the photograph. Finally, on the left, there's a fake tree trunk that is actually a streetlamp.

CHAPTER TWO

Milan. Il Grillo. Prison.
Tortoreto. Return to Tortoreto.
Palas Street in Bucharest.

No SOONER HAD I ARRIVED IN MILAN THAN I was struck by the fact, not of being in Italy or at the university, but of being alone. Solitude was my deepest experience at that time: the discovery and novelty of solitude, its pleasures and terrors. I lived in Italy for eight years, and yet I didn't see all that much of it; even in Milan I got to know only a particular neighborhood. My chief interest just then was in girls. What I was looking for was love, to find myself through love. I was always out, I never stayed home. I couldn't study or concentrate or read. After the war I went back to revisit the battlefield, to see the things I hadn't seen when I first lived there, and to recapture the emotions of those years. You understand things in a different way the second time around, you understand them truly and digest them. We are like ruminants, who in order to digest have to pass their food through more than one stomach.

In the spring of 1940, shortly before Italy entered the war, I expected to be arrested. I knew the arrest would take place between six and seven o'clock in the morning. They did it that way because, as Solzhenitsyn tells us, arrests are carried out in the "antisocial" hours when society is asleep. In Russia, naturally, at two in the morning, and I'm sure it was the same in Germany with the Nazis. In Italy, they made their arrests at a more civilized hour, for the benefit of the cops, poor guys, who had to get up at five, drink a coffee, and still half-asleep go and brutally rouse other folks out of bed, so that people in corridors and streets wouldn't see what was going on.

For some weeks I had been waking up a little before six, and as soon as I'd washed my face I jumped on my bicycle and rode through the streets like a man on his way to work. The air in Milan was excellent at that time, and the light beautiful, and I saw something I had never seen before, the calm and silent awakening of a city: people on foot, people on bicycles, trams, workers. I got home after seven, and it was absolutely certain that if they hadn't come by seven o'clock they weren't coming. (Saturdays and Sundays they never came.) I had breakfast and went back to bed to sleep a while longer, and I had the great satisfaction of a whole free day ahead of me—more than a vacation, almost a life gained.

I lived at Il Grillo, a bar close to the university that rented a few rooms to students. One morning, just as I was about to go down to the street as I did every day, the youngest of the four sisters who owned the bar came very anxiously into my room: "They're here, downstairs."

Luckily there was a way to get out through the courtyard without being seen.

When I got back at eight, after telephoning to be sure they'd left, I was welcomed like a hero, like someone who'd had a narrow escape. They told me that one of

MILAN ITALY

the policemen, like a real Sherlock Holmes, had felt the bed and said, "It's still warm."

The policemen were poor devils, southerners who did this job without taking any interest in it. But their laziness, the fact that the organization did not function well, resulted in an inefficiency that would then be converted into a lack of injustice.

I spent almost a year clandestinely, sleeping sometimes at Il Grillo, sometimes in the studio of friends, and meanwhile I was able to get the visas I needed. The only one missing was the Italian one, which they wouldn't issue without my physical presence, proof of having obeyed the law.

I had to turn myself in. With my arrest, my dossier was legally completed and settled. I was running a risk, but it was the only thing to do, so I did it and it worked. I have a touch of amnesia concerning that time: I was experiencing an emotion that covered my eyes, ears, all my senses with a sort of padding, so as to conceal the gravity of the situation from myself. I felt as though I were playing a part, seeing myself as though I were someone else, something like the situation of a man drawing a picture of a man—a symptom perhaps of persistent childhood, which doesn't end and of which one is never cured.

As soon as I was put in prison I saw myself as an important character. In history, all important characters have gone to prison. At San Vittore, which is a classical prison, I had to undergo the classical treatment of people who end up in prison: off with the belt and whatever you have in your pockets, which to begin with means a loss of dignity—your pants fall down. The second thing is cohabitation with excrement, since the pot is in common. As cellmates I had two bicycle thieves, individuals of little importance, whose excuse was that they stole bicycles out of hunger. Since I told them I'd been locked up for more or less political reasons, all of a sudden they were afraid and didn't want to have anything to do with me. The second day I was put in a cell with another political detainee, or perhaps a false detainee who was there as a stool pigeon or for some other reason.

Because I was young, this was all a great adventure for me. I liked to think I was participating in life in such an intense fashion: I wasn't just a reader of novels but a real hero, as I'd always wished. And I saw the moment come true when the dream becomes reality.

A pair of cops took me to the station in Milan and put me on the train for the Abruzzi. Two friends had come to see me off, Donizetti and Aldo, and a girlfriend named Ada. Donizetti brought me some medicine—quinine, I think—for malaria. This, too, was happiness: I had a woman who loved me and two friends. Before that I'd had only my family—that is to say, people I had neither invented nor found for myself.

In the compartment I was alone with the two policemen, who tried to keep other passengers out. But right away I had become an object of curiosity because they realized I was being taken to prison, and the girls were especially interested. They stood there watching. For women a prisoner is a romantic, adventurous character, who has done something unlawful and thus might even do something unlawful to them, or rather for them. Moreover, I was a foreigner, young, and also looked underfed. Admired and desired by those girls, I felt perfect.

During that wonderful trip I saw perilous mountains for the first time, with the train going ever so slowly along the edge of the abyss, which was precisely my situation. At a certain point—it was spring and Easter was coming—a procession of penitents, who had made a pilgrimage on their knees, boarded the train. They were all ecstatic and sang in fine, very loud voices. The train shook with these songs.

We arrived in Tortoreto, in the Abruzzi, after two days of traveling, sleeping on benches in stations, and changing trains. The "camp" was a villa from which you could see the sea, but you weren't allowed to go to it. The camp was small, with perhaps fifty internees: a few Jews, White Russians, gypsies, stateless persons, refugees, being held there in a fairly makeshift and human fashion as compared with other camps. I was lucky.

One of the prisoners was an Austrian violinist with an odd name: Aloysius Gogg (Gog and Magog, Van Gogh), a good-humored man whose faith was inexhaustible. For almost a year he had hidden out in an inn near Genoa with the innkeeper's consent, provided he make love to the wife, who was young and needed it. The innkeeper preferred to have a man in the house who was clean and under his control, rather than letting his wife roam the streets, picking up dirty young rough-necks.

Like me, Aloysius Gogg had turned up in this place so as to be able to leave Italy legally, and we left together. The day they told us we were being freed, our com-panions offered us a special supper. They brought out whatever good things they could—lots of bread and the sweetest tea. Gogg played the violin, but with a mute and in the dark, since we weren't allowed to keep the light on after nine o'clock. The next day everyone saw us off as far as the corner of the station. The two of us and a guard went into the station and the others stood and watched us. Then they ran back.

When our train left Tortoreto and passed behind the camp, we saw them again. From the roof and windows of the villa they were waving to us with sheets and towels, anything that was white and could be waved.

Later I saw Gogg again in America; we saw each other a couple of times. He was very glad I had managed to get to New York and been successful in my work. What he was doing I couldn't tell—he spoke vaguely. In the end they put him in uniform, like me, but in the army. And then he changed his name. I think he took the name Warner. When the war was over, I made inquiries to see what had happened to him, but I found out nothing.

In 1944 I was back in Italy in the uniform of an American naval officer, and in Bari I saw one of my fellow detainees again, but he didn't recognize me. To make a living, he was selling stamps at a stand on the street: Nazi stamps, which were already rare, and some even rarer ones, which I bought from him, Italian stamps of the former regime and Fascism, with the figure of the king and an overprinting in red. I asked him a few questions, as if I were a Jew from America taking an interest in another Jew, how he'd escaped, and so on. He told me, "As soon as Mussolini fell, we were freed, and luckily I went south. Others, poor things, went north."

———

The main meal at Tortoreto was bread and tea—tea because there was no coffee. You can always find tea in Italy because nobody drinks it. Instead of sugar we used a little honey, or a piece of candy. Even bread was a sort of sugar, because it becomes sweetish when dipped in tea. There was quite a traffic in bread: fresh bread, dry bread, all kinds of bread. Grass and herbs, a bit of onion, were added to make bread soup, bread pies. The pope gave us six lire a day as an allowance, and for his own peace of mind. Luckily I was there in May; it was warm, there was the fine spring sunshine, and already they were starting to find greens, lots of onions. I even saw a dog eating onions, a dog who lived with us and didn't know he was in a concentration camp.

The women of Tortoreto had stepped right out of the Byzantine mosaics in Ravenna. They had round eyes (eyes like the ones I saw later in the comic strips: Mickey Mouse, Orphan Annie . . .), with an incredible stare and eyebrows as thick as mustaches, and very taut skin, which looked stuffed to the point of bursting, of a color verging on copper. On their heads they carried large copper water jugs, and they walked with dignity, as though they were bearing the world on their heads. They were very curious about these young foreigners whom they were seeing for the first time (the invasions of armies and tourism still lay in the future). They stared at us passionately, also because while they were looking, they couldn't turn their heads due to the weight that was on them. I could almost see the rays, the fire, that came from their eyes. Added to that was the desire one felt because of abstinence, a desire equally strong on both sides, for it was clear that the girls were truly virgins full of passion. It could also be seen from all those bulging curves ready to explode: bosoms, back sides, and so forth, forms and dimensions of a vigor seldom to be seen, and which stood out even more starkly because of the modesty and color of their clothes—between brown and black.

Years later, in 1957, I went back to see those places once more. I was anxious: I wanted to go and didn't want to go;

I was afraid of spoiling the memory, and I wanted to spoil it. And I succeeded.

Arriving in Tortoreto, I had to drive along the main street, which was full of people, unlike in Fascist times. The village had become Communist, and since elections were coming up there was a lot of unrest. They looked at me with hostility, because I was traveling in an automobile they'd never seen, and because I was a stranger. They got out of the car's way grudgingly so as to demonstrate their right to occupy the street, and already this looked to me like a bad omen for the hero returning free and triumphant.

Finally I found myself in front of the villa. It had been renovated, fixed up and painted pink—flowers everywhere. It looked as though it was inhabited by rich landowners, who in Italy usually live behind walls with glass shards on them. The place seemed horrible to me, and I went away without getting out of the car.

A little later I discovered that it wasn't the real Tortoreto, but Tortoreto Nereto, which meant that the villa was not the one where I had been confined. It had looked a little different to me, but I'd thought it was due to the passage of time: fifteen years.

This mistake saved me. Leaving Tortoreto Nereto, I came to a road where a sign said TORTORETO STAZIONE, and from there I could see the place where I used to take walks. I had no trouble recognizing it, but I didn't go any closer.

I didn't want to, just as I don't want to go back to Romania: they are places that don't belong to geography but to time. And the memory of these places of sadness, of suffering, but above all of great emotions, is spoiled by seeing them again. It's better to leave certain things in peace, just the way they are in memory: with the passage of time they become the mythology of our lives. I haven't even wanted to see certain people again with whom I had been more or less friendly in terms of time and place: schoolmates, childhood companions. You can't resume a dialogue that never was a real dialogue but rather a temporary complicity, the kind of complicity established among people occupying the same compartment in a train. Of course, if I had to go back and live on

Palas Street in Bucharest, where I spent my childhood and youth, yes, I would do it; but to pay the place a hasty visit would seem to me an inadmissible lack of respect.

Palas Street was my homeland, a little street completely apart from traffic. Grass grew on it, and I believe still does. I gave directions to a friend who was going to Romania and he brought me back not only color photos but also slides to project on the wall, in color and almost life-size. They moved me deeply, especially since nothing has changed except for some trees, which have grown taller, and a wall that's now covered with ivy. I was horrified to see an automobile in the courtyard of my house. The street looks more tawdry because where there were gas lamps there are now huge wooden poles. Moreover, they've done something completely pointless: on a little street at most eight or nine meters wide, they've painted white stripes on the pavement at the pedestrian crossings.

I felt as though I were peering into a tomb, lifting the sheet from a corpse. I felt angry as well as curious to see, and then angry for having seen—as though I had lost something.

Later I calmed down, and to cure myself of this illness I sent two other friends to take pictures. One of them took the same pictures, but in winter with snow, which was more beautiful because the changes were less obvious. The other took a detail I wanted: the courtyard seen through the gate, the house number and plate. All the same as ever, all the same, except that fifty years have passed.

CHAPTER THREE

Washington, Smithsonian Institution.
Baseball. Hillbillies. Traveling by bus.
Bums, the Bowery. The American Dream.
The influence of Cubism.
Magritte. American restaurants.

IN WASHINGTON IN 1966, AS AN ARTIST-IN-RESIDENCE at the Smithsonian Institution, I spent perhaps the strangest three months of my life. It was as though I'd emigrated to a place where normally no one emigrates— Norway, say, or Albania. In New York you might meet Senator Javits and that was all. In Washington I met the chief figures in American politics: cabinet officials, secretaries of state, former secretaries of state such as Acheson, famous newspapermen, ambassadors. And their wives, all perfectly trained in drawing-room life, how to receive, how to make polite conversation, how to be attractive; they're brought up in finishing schools for young ladies—these are especially in the South—or maybe sent to boarding schools in Lausanne where they learn to eat with six forks. Women brought up to be ladies: they know how to give orders to the cook but they don't know either how to cook or to eat with an appetite because that's against the rules. They know exactly how to be courteous, to entertain, to put people at their ease, but also how to get rid of people who may not necessarily be boring but are boring at the moment, people who don't belong to the group, or who need to be dismissed a little earlier.

The colonel's wife is prepared to be nasty and give orders to the wife of the captain or lieutenant. Who knows what they really talk about with their husbands? Everything happens in a superficial way, like in a B movie. They look like faithful and loving couples, they keep in shape physically, and the only signs of age are when their hair turns white and invisible wrinkles appear—always like made-up actors in a film.

It was against this world that the hippie revolution of nudity, and especially of violence, took place.

I was invited to important dinners, which were staged according to all the rules for official occasions, with each guest's name written by calligraphy specialists to indicate the place at table. A diagram of the table with the seating arrangement was on view at the entrance, so each person knew who would be sitting to his right and to his left, with the obligation to escort the lady assigned to him into the dining room. The lady on the left or the one on the right? I don't remember anymore.

I learned to eat with several forks and drink from several glasses, not to drink the water in the finger bowl or eat certain fruits and vegetables that were there as simple decoration, and not to take the apple from the pig's mouth. I almost always wore a black tie, a white shirt, and gold cuff links—which I've never worn since.

I lived in Georgetown, in a magnificent house that looked like a Danish palace. It belonged to a zoologist who specialized in the large anthropoid apes, with the result that in his library I learned a lot about gorillas. Above the staircase hung the huge stuffed head of an African water buffalo, the animal that caused the death of young Macomber in Hemingway's story. Going up the stairs I didn't see it, but coming down it was right in front of me, looking me straight in the eye. A horror. But I couldn't ask them to take it away.

The servants were four Chinese: father, mother, and two daughters. The house, with four floors, needed a lot of attention: hundreds of chairs, cutlery services, chinoiseries. The father was also the cook, but his cooking was lousy—the worst beefsteak I've ever eaten. He was a Chinese cook who cooked badly, just as there are short Swedes. I had him make only hard-boiled eggs and toast. Besides, he was a thief: he presented me with huge bills. I was well paid, but I was determined not to save so much as a penny and even to pay a lot out of my own pocket so as not to feel too indebted to the government, and to uphold my honor as a guest of the Smithsonian. Every evening I was asked out. I had to refuse many attractive invitations from important senators and intelligent congressmen, since there were others that I absolutely couldn't turn down. Washington at that time was a fairly gloomy place because of the war in Vietnam. President Lyndon Johnson was unpopular. We met in homes a little in the way we met in air-raid shelters during the war.

There were also nice, intelligent, well-informed women. A pity they were courtiers, like everyone in Washington—the opposite of peasants, of frank and sincere people.

The Smithsonian's stationery was very beautiful, with perfect steel engravings on various qualities of paper, each more deluxe than the next. I did many drawings on these sheets of paper, using the letterhead in various ways.* Furthermore, perhaps influenced by the servants, I drew a Chinese type scroll thirty feet long, on which I developed a continuous drawing, based on what I did each day: a diary in drawings. The danger is that you become enslaved to the scroll, and in the end I ruined it by trying to make it beautiful. But a few feet survived.

* These drawings went to make a book: *Steinberg at the Smithsonian—The Metamorphosis of an Emblem*, preface by John Hollander, published by the National Collection of Fine Arts of the Smithsonian Institution Press, Washington, D.C., 1973.

———

Washington is like an ocean liner, the *Queen Mary* or the *Queen Elizabeth*. By living in Georgetown I was in first class, so to speak. Second class? The government employees. Tourist class means the tourists, and of course the blacks are the crew who take care of everything for the passengers.

Each is on board for a four-year voyage, which is how long an administration lasts. Each wants to be invited to the captain's table, although the less fortunate will eat with the purser.

When the voyage is coming to an end, things get worse: baggage, waiters, porters appear on deck, and the ship is cleaned up for a new batch of passengers.*

The first time I attended a baseball game I understood nothing, but still I was curious about this game where

* From "Steinberg Looks at Washington," interview with Karl E. Mayer, *The Washington Post*, March 15, 1970. The thought was expressed in the source cited and is paraphrased here.

there's almost no action and yet people watch it with great expectation and emotion. Baseball is a philosophical, psychological sport, based, like life, on courage and fear—think of chess and bullfighting. The players have to have extraordinary ability, ready reflexes, and above all an inventive spirit, a creativity that might be called poetic and which puts the sports champion close to the artist. The great players don't want to look like athletes but rather like businessmen; and they show a kind of indifference toward their ability; they don't talk about baseball. Likewise, neither do good painters, while the mediocre ones dress like artists and talk of nothing but art.

During the 1954 season I followed the Milwaukee Braves in Philadelphia, Chicago, Cincinnati, Milwaukee, and other cities. Baseball stadiums today are more refined, better cared for, created more for large spectacles. They even put a plastic dome on top of one of them, as protection against sun and rain. Some of the grass is artificial, while in those days all of it was still real. The old stadiums, especially the one in Philadelphia, or Ebbets Field in New York, were fantastic architectural structures of wood that gave you the feeling you were seeing a naval disaster of the nineteenth century, a collision of big riverboats.

In the early summer of 1958 I went to Kentucky and West Virginia to visit the hillbillies, the poor whites, who have always interested me because they are somewhat the ancestors of today's Americans. In them I saw many protagonists of American fiction, characters out of Faulkner, movie heroes, cowboys, thieves, tramps—the real American characters. The bourgeoisie, respectable people, they're everywhere and always the same.

Traveling by train, you see most of all the back side of cities. The view is "lateral," while for man the most natural view is the front one, as in an automobile. Except that in a car you sit too low, so low you're afraid of scraping your ass on the road. And you see a landscape that is the continuation of the one on television, which indeed you see while sitting down.

Traveling by bus, if you manage to sit in the first row, you enjoy the ideal view, the rarest and most noble one, the view of the man on horseback. Now, unfortunately, they've started tinting the windows against the sun and you see a sad crepuscular landscape, even if there's bright sunlight. Or else they color the windshield blue, shading it toward the bottom, and thus the panorama is transformed into a Japanese print.

Here there is every sort of *felicità*, including the horrendous happiness of Florida, concentration camps for old people, the happiness of the rich, who want only to buy things, and the happiness of the bums, the human wrecks. In every large city there's a place called skid row (in New York, it's the Bowery), which is the free zone for derelicts and drunkards, people who want to end their lives in their own way, looking for happiness until the end according to their own judgment, even if they're idiots or lunatics. As long as they don't bother others too much, the police leave them alone. When winter comes they arrest them all and put them in jail, just to keep them warm, so they don't freeze to death. When they quarrel among themselves, the weakness caused by alcoholism makes them fight in slow motion, with slow and feeble gestures, and when they strike a blow it doesn't hurt, each falls down while trying to hit the other. They stave off sadness with cheap wine. Almost all of them die young. Sometimes you see a fairly old one who has managed to live a great part of his life among bums, or else he may have joined their ranks only recently. There are those who work steadily for years, businessmen with families, and all of a sudden they enter the skid-row world, and prefer to spend the rest of their lives there. Suicide, except it takes a little longer.

On the Bowery you see many noble faces, marked by life's sufferings, but without the degradation of vulgarity and cunning. There are artists there, painters (I'm not talking about musicians or writers, who don't belong to the same family), defenseless, childish creatures who use their intelligence and courage not for survival, who are primarily concerned with their integrity; who don't exploit anyone, or live on this earth like those who are born with a specific purpose and think of life as something from which to gain the greatest possible advantage. The face of Ulysses S. Grant, president of the United States, which appears on the fifty-dollar bill, to me represents, in a moving way, the artist and the derelict.

The American Dream is the ideal offered to us by the Constitution, that of seeking happiness all one's life. It is an invitation to use all the facilities offered by America—this country where one has the opportunity to respect good laws—to pursue one's tendencies freely and seek happiness as one thinks best. There's no such thing as a standard happiness, the same for everyone. Happiness is not imposed on Americans from outside, by the government, as happens under dictatorships.

On the Bowery the Salvation Army is always present to offer food, warmth, and cleanliness. What it asks in return is that you listen to a sermon and sing. But many refuse: they don't want to hear the sermon and they don't want to sing; they prefer to beg or steal rather than do something that goes against their nature.

As soon as I arrived in New York, one of the things that immediately struck me was the great influence of Cubism on American architecture. And Art Deco was merely the decline of Cubism's influence, Cubism turned decorative: the Chrysler Building, the Empire State Building, jukeboxes, cafeterias, shops, women's dresses and hairdos, men's neckties—everything was created out of Cubist elements. The taxis, much bigger than they are now, were built precisely to be taxis: six, seven, eight people could fit in them; there was a sliding panel in the roof, so that from inside you could see the tall skyscrapers and at night the moon—it was something beautiful, which, as often happens, all of a sudden ended without anyone protesting. Each taxi company had its own insignia, its own colors, a fine mixture of reds, greens, dark greens, of black-and-white checkers, very shiny enamel colors. The word "taxi" was in plastic, lit from within, and belonging to the same family as the jukeboxes of the time, with yellow, red, and orange lights. The influence of Constructivism, of Cubism, and,

if you like, of Fernandlégerism, was obvious: the automobile gave the impression of going at great speed even
when it was standing still. De Soto (taxis were Dodges
and De Sotos, I think) had as a hood ornament a flying
Indian that derived directly from Brancusi and his flying
birds. All this ended after the war, and people embarked
on other ways of dressing, other forms of architecture. A
decline, because it was really a very American world, and
very optimistic.

soon met the celebrities of the place: Chagall, Max
Ernst, Léger, Duchamp; and our natives, Pollock, de
Kooning, John Graham . . . I'm sorry not to have met
Mondrian. Magritte arrived here very late. I liked some
of his things, but in general I thought he worked too hard
at painting just to explain a joke. But that was his real talent, or rather his true discovery as a loyal soldier of
Surrealism: working with the same meticulousness and
passion that miniaturists employed in illuminating the
codexes. Magritte became famous in America only in his
last years.

I have one of the earlier Magrittes, from 1926, one of his best, I think, and well painted with that famous patience. It's a double portrait of André Breton: two profiles, one saying *"Le piano"* and the other answering *"La violette."* The speech balloons coming out of the two mouths are of a dense and opaque salmon-violet color, and are fairly elongated in shape. Maybe in choosing this color, Magritte meant to show a continuation of the two tongues. It's probably a joke on the comic strips. Also, the painting represents the back of an oil painting. Magritte painted on it, in a dark brown color, almost black, the outline of the stretcher (another Surrealist joke), which would be the back of the painting itself, or rather the painting seen transparently, from behind.

I bought it from my dealer, Sidney Janis, who owed me four hundred dollars. Instead of the money I took this painting, which had been in the show organized by Janis after mine, a show at which Magritte sold nothing, or maybe just one painting. It was a good deal for Janis— at that time.

Magritte discovered the three sources of light (and

maybe a few more). In a painting of which he did several variants, you see the sky illuminated by the last reflections of the sunset, while the other elements of the landscape, a tree, a house, are dark silhouettes against the sky. On the street there's a streetlamp, already on, which illuminates part of the street and part of the house. In the house the electric light is on, illuminating the interior and shining through to the outside: three lights. There's a moon, I think, which is already starting to cast a little light. And I'm almost certain that he also painted a light reflected in a puddle, or maybe one sees a little bit of the sea.

Magritte was much attached to these curious effects. In America, Edward Hopper was a very skillful specialist in neon light. He painted highway scenes at sunset where, with the usual waste in America, one sees the neon lights already lit, the lights of the street, the lights of restaurants, gas stations, and the headlights of automobiles heading toward a dazzling sunset.

The idea of painting light is a good one, because it makes the artist a magician, someone who is able to re-create light with paint alone. But, of course, that's not the function of painting; Magritte spoke less as an artist than as a scientist or, more modestly, a technician.

In America you don't ask passersby to point out a good restaurant, as you do in Italy or France. People don't understand what a good restaurant is, because here one goes to a restaurant not to eat but to have a good time. To answer, they'd have to know why you want to go: to pick up a girl, to take the family and have an unforgettable evening with music and soft lights, to gorge yourself or have a quick snack. They wouldn't even be able to say whether some diner is good or bad: a diner is a diner. People go to the diner in Watermill because there's lots of room and you're served quickly. There's another restaurant nearby that's a different matter entirely: you have to dress properly, spend a couple of hours—it's a big deal. And you have to take your time eating and spend a lot of money. It's the place to take someone you want to impress. If you're a family with children, you go to a diner, what around here is called a greasy spoon, where you eat a plate of fried stuff—the stuff kids like. Gastronomy in America, the restaurants, the taste of the nation are governed by the tastes of children. This is a disaster, because children would prefer to eat nothing but spaghetti, hamburgers, and hot dogs. Spaghetti they eat with meatballs, drowned in sauce and soft as mush; they love hamburgers with the roll drenched in hamburger juice, smothered with ketchup, and with French fries that have been deep-fried in bad-smelling fats. Let's not talk about frankfurters, hot dogs: they may even be quite good, but not around here, with the worst kind of mustard. But that's how kids like them.

The young people who are coming up now have preserved the behavior and habits of the nursery, the playroom, the kindergarten. Due to the mistaken influence of Freud, who taught that children shouldn't be given complexes, they've never been scolded; the people around them have shown them the utmost patience. Occasionally you hear of children being strangled: probably by mothers or fathers who have been patient too long and have ended by delivering the scolding all at once.

These young people have been fed nonstop, and have never lost the taste for eating at all times, first forced by their mothers, then by the schools with their free lunches, where they eat what they want and buy anything that's available, always surrounded by advertisements for things made especially for them: horrible sweets, pizzas, hamburgers, ice cream. On their way home from school they go on eating and drinking in the street: in one hand they hold a slice of pizza wrapped in paper, in the other an aluminum can with a straw sticking out of it, or even two or three straws so they can suck it up quicker. They pause at street corners to talk or look around. When they've finished their drink, they spread their fingers and the empty can falls on the ground. They don't even look at it, like cows letting their shit fall in a meadow. When they finish their pizza, they drop the paper in the same way, or even a piece of pizza they don't want. If you reprove them they look at you as if you were crazy. They don't understand. If you're unlucky, you may even run into one who'll kill you for making remarks that he's not used to hearing. In their rooms at home, they've made every sort of mess on the floor, dirt, vomit, and worse. You often see on television a room reduced to a pigsty where a patient mother is showing off the appliance that cleans it all up in a minute. The child is proud to have made this demonstration of the product's worth possible. Since it's so easy to clean things up, he has never been scolded for dirtying his room, and therefore he intends to spend the rest of his life behaving in the same way.

To ask a passerby where you can get a good meal is like asking him about his social class, or what his political interests are—an embarrassing question because going to a restaurant is a social, not a gastronomical matter. In New York, as you know, with so many foreigners and all kinds of restaurants, the situation is not typical of America. I've been to a large restaurant in Cincinnati where there was an ice-skating rink at the center with variety numbers: a skater took a ballerina by the hands and swung her around in circles more and more rapidly, with her skates aimed toward my mouth, which was open for eating. The place was full of families with children, banquet tables to celebrate a birthday, the children with funny hats on their heads. Here was a restaurant with music, entertainment, special lights, not one restful moment for eating. If you ordered a salad, what they brought you were old lettuce leaves—an encyclopedia would have been just as good, an old encyclopedia, or pages from the phone book. The meat dishes were all the same, with different names, even French ones.

When I had a studio on Sixtieth Street, I could see two restaurants from my window: the Veau d'Or on Sixtieth, and another French restaurant on Sixty-first. In the courtyard between them was a kitchen that served both restaurants, and the cooks were Chinese.

The only really good meal here is breakfast. When I traveled I ate breakfast at noon, too, and in the evening. A coffee and a local Danish pastry, or even some agreeable novelties. Ham or bacon and well-cooked eggs with toast. This dish comes with tasty home-fried potatoes, cooked with bacon and onion, or with French fries, on which you put ketchup. Raw ham doesn't exist, but the cooked kind is excellent: Virginia ham with pineapple, smoked ham from the South, or Canadian bacon, which is a cross between bacon and ham. And sausages, and crisp waffles, imprinted by hot irons, which look like the backside of someone who's been sitting without his trousers on a straw-bottomed chair, and you eat them with maple syrup, or with honey or jam; and flapjacks, soft pancakes made from white flour, cornmeal, or rye flour. You order them by the stack, a skyscraper; you spread them with butter, honey, syrup, or jam; you put three or four on top of one another and cut them like sandwiches, swallowing mouthfuls like a crocodile.

In small agricultural towns on the plains (Kansas, Iowa), where you get the best waffles and flapjacks, the diners are enormous, with big tables. It's a pleasure to sit, even by yourself, at a big table. If there are two of you, it's delightful to sit at a table for four or six. The waitresses are very nice and always prompt, not like in New York or here at the seashore, especially in summer, when the waitresses are students, and serving in the restaurants you may find angry whores, jilted sweethearts, poisoners, and even worse, women without the slightest interest in what they're doing or what they're serving. These towns instead are places with real waitresses (of course not all of the women are waitresses, but all of them could be), and all of them, young or not, look pleasantly maternal. Since there's not much to do, they enjoy themselves and care about giving their customers good service. Here not only are the restaurants, tables, and chairs big, but so are the flapjacks and other dishes: everything has heroic dimensions and doesn't cost much.

In Italy you look for restaurants frequented by truck drivers; in America it's better to follow trainmen—more polite, less violent people, who don't drink too much. Truck drivers have a cowboy mentality, they sometimes show off their masculinity by eating horrible and indigestible dishes such as chili con carne, or else huge quantities of food, slops, pailfuls of dirty water, like the ones that rained down in the street from the balconies in Romania.

The diner is one of the most elegant, most pleasant, most American places. Born during the Depression, it was originally a real railway car or tram. Little by little it was enlarged, while keeping, however, its architectural structure and covering it with stamped aluminum, a material that for ordinary people suggests luxury, the equivalent of the mirrors, brass, mahogany, and colored glass windows of restaurants in France at the end of the last century. In a certain sense it is a childish luxury, but just right for me, since I feel ill at ease in places that are too elegant. The diner is even the American equivalent of the Brasserie Lipp in Paris. The aluminum is stamped in shapes often derived from Cubism, and symbolizing the speed of the train and the poetic or worldly or modern qualities of the setting. For a restaurant it's perfect: it's hygienic and easy to keep clean; it reflects without blinding you the neon lights decorating it; and gives prominence to the jukebox, which is built according to the laws of the Catholic or Chinese or Hindu altar, a magical object to be worshiped because all good things come from it: music, dance, love, and joy.

In the diner you can sit at the counter to eat quickly, without taking off your hat, or if you prefer, take a seat, alone or accompanied, in one of the booths, which are very comfortable because they are spacious, the tables covered with Formica that is always kept clean, and with a little army of helpers in front of you: the paper-napkin holders, salt, pepper, ketchup, mustard, and so on. Too bad there are no more toothpicks—now they're at the cashier's desk, where you pay the bill. Furthermore, at every table there's a slot where you can put in a dime or quarter: you press the button and the jukebox plays whatever you like. Ideal places. There's always a lovely view outside: a parking lot, a road full of traffic, or some backyard with unexpected sights; or else a motel.

CHAPTER FOUR

Drawing from life.
Reflections, shadows.
The cartoonist's profession.
Selling my work. The art world.
The carpenter Sig Lomaky.

As an architecture student I made an excellent study tour with my school to Ferrara and Rome. It was there that for the first time I did drawings from life. I, who have had no professional artistic training and have learned to draw by drawing, had so far thought mostly of imaginary drawings, things you invent. During that trip, I realized how hard it is to do a drawing from life, and how important to understand the nature, the truth of reality. To understand the truth of the drawing's subject matter—people, architecture, or landscape—is a complex thing since it isn't a visible, superficial truth. And it takes a lot of effort, a dedication that sometimes, out of laziness, one strives to avoid (it's easier to invent). You must manage to establish complicity with whatever you're drawing, until you gain a deep knowledge of it. You don't draw well if you're telling a lie. And conversely, when a drawing from life tells the truth, it automatically turns out to be a good drawing. Another problem in drawing from life is that we're obliged to find answers to questions that so far haven't been raised. The work you do in the studio is often an answer to questions that are already familiar.

It's hard to do a portrait. You must first spend a critical moment in which you quickly—if you're lucky—discard all the commonplaces about the subject of the drawing. More difficult than inventing is giving up accumulated virtues. The things you discovered yesterday are no longer valid. It's impossible to find anything new without first giving something up.

There's a moral in this. It's stinginess that holds us back, especially when we're not only enamored of what we've discovered but also convinced it's good. There are those who, in working from life, continually use the bag-

gage they picked up yesterday; they work from life without really looking, without working from life.

Why am I so reluctant to draw from life, and why do
I look for any excuse not to? It's hard to tell the truth
about anything, or to portray oneself in terms of something else. What I try to do is to say with painting something more than what the eye sees. My paintings are not
so much paintings in themselves as parts of a table,
objects of a drawing table, the painter's work table. The
pencils and other things I do are there to say that this is
not a painting of mine but a painting by someone else,
maybe a painting by "that painter" but not by me. In that
case, I'm more an orchestra conductor than a painter
doing a painting. My work says something about something else; if it's painting it says something about painting, not about the fact that this is what it is. If I use a
rubber stamp on the painting, I do it to show that this
paint is not real paint, it's a symbol of the thing painted,
just as the stamp is a symbol of the man. I'm not sure
whether this is a sign of modesty or the reverse.

My development started at the bottom, with cartoons. I learned by working and I managed to get out of a

number of culs-de-sac, some of the vulgarities of humorous drawing and the banalities of commercial art, while still preserving a little of that element of mediocrity—I'd almost say vulgarity—that I wouldn't care to give up, since I consider it something necessary; like a man who, in changing his social class, still wouldn't want to break up with his wife and old friends.

A drawing from life reveals too much of me. In other drawings—those done from the imagination—I do only what I want and show myself and my world in the way I choose. But in drawing from life, I am no longer the protagonist; I become a kind of servant, a second-class character. I am so propelled by the reality in front of me that I forget myself and work as though in a trance, trying to single out the reality, doing the drawing without realizing I'm doing it. And so I'm afraid that the drawing reveals certain parts of myself, areas of vulgarity where I don't tell the truth, making use of what I already know, commonplaces, and I see in myself—I mean in the drawing I've done—some of my regular faults: stopping without finishing, getting tired at a certain moment and failing to insist on some point that ought instead to be essential; out of timidity or laziness I don't insist, and so things don't end the way they should—the result doesn't live up to the promise. Sometimes there's a touch of something seductive in what I do, which would be fine if I followed through, if I kept the promise.

Once a drawing from life is done, I can't help taking it up again later, to check everything in cold blood and add the finishing touches. Only when a lot of time has passed do I look at these drawings again, not with the critical eye I had originally, but rather with a father's benevolence for his child. But I'm always suspicious of what I've done without my own blessing. I'm just the opposite of an Expressionist. And also of an Impressionist, if you like.

In 1950 I did drawings more or less from life of American landscapes, streets in America, things by now vanished. No one at the time took an interest in these things; American painters were looking for places, corners, that looked like "real painting"; even on Main Street they looked for a little bit of English painting or something out of Rembrandt or Vermeer. There were a number of painters in New York—Reginald Marsh, for example—who looked for Hogarths or Rubenses on Fourteenth Street. Art bloomed here in America primarily because of the lack of attention paid to it. When in 1940 the great season of American painting began, one thing that certainly influenced art was poverty, which forced artists to create their own working space. They took cold-water flats and transformed them into studios, and to make them livable they had to scrape and paint the walls, doors and windows, and floors. Gifted painters had to turn into house painters and this led them to work on a large scale, to use industrial paints, such as gold or silver on radiators, new materials. The studio was no longer a place that got northern exposure. You worked, especially in the city, at night or even in the daytime, in the bright illumination of neon lighting.

The idea of reflections came to me in reading an observation by Pascal, cited in a book by W. H. Auden, who wrote an unusual kind of autobiography by collecting all the quotations he had annotated in the course of his life, which is a good way of displaying oneself, as a reflection of these quotations. Among them this observation by Pascal, which could have been made only by a mathematician: that the symmetry of the human body, its external symmetry of course, is horizontal. In nature this horizontal symmetry also exists in animals and plants, but in nature at large, which is the scene of life, the nature of the earth and sky, there exists only a vertical symmetry, produced by water, nature's mirror.

Water was man's first mirror. It was an inconvenient mirror—man saw himself against the sky and against the light. So, since he couldn't take the water and hang it on the wall, he had to invent the mirror in order to look at himself.

What you see in reverse in the reflection is almost always better than the original—for color, sharpness, intensity, and intelligibility. Venice, where vertical and horizontal reflections coexist, is a perfect example of art and nature combined, since architecture, which is all horizontal symmetry, becomes vertical symmetry when reflected in water.

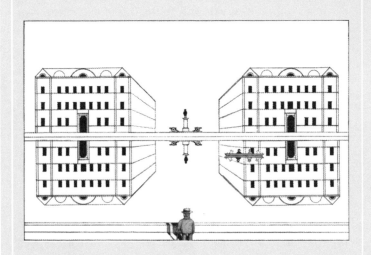

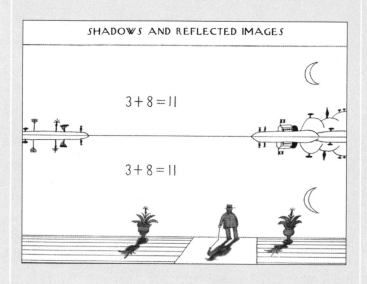

There is also an equivalence between landscape and the way it is reflected in clouds: a form of reflection of nature. In the Navajo desert in Arizona, with its gigantic formations of red rocks, the clouds take on equally monumental forms. Lakes also produce their specific clouds. But this would be less a visual phenomenon than a form of symmetry. . . . It's easier for me to draw these things than to explain them.

I did a drawing that represents what I might call different degrees of reality. A woman is crossing a bridge, a semi-oval bridge like the kind in Venice, and she's carrying a jug on her head. Jug and woman are one on top of the other and reversed. Thus either the woman is a reflection of the jug, or the jug is a reflection of the woman. And these two pseudo-reflections are reflected in the water, where the woman's legs are up and her head down, resting on the jug. If the woman is a real woman, the jug can be considered a woman-once-removed. . . .

The reflection in itself is a second-degree reality, because it is not real but only produced by the real object. What interest me here are the differences between first-, second-, third-, and fourth-degree realities.

In the same drawing I copied a famous painting by George Caleb Bingham, *Fur Traders Descending the Missouri*, complete with reflections in the water of the river, cat, and all. It's a question of still another degree of reality, perhaps a third or fourth degree, because it's not real and, what's more, this pseudo-reality is reflected not in its own water—which would be the one in the painting—but in mine, I mean the one drawn by me.

In the reflection of the boat there is something that doesn't figure in Bingham's painting: a duck, which I drew, a more advanced reality, more important than the painting and its reflection. Of course, this duck, too, has its own reflection in the water.

These reflections enchant me by the strangeness of their existence (strangeness is a quality of miracles). Sinyavsky says that verses, rhymes, are very appropriate instruments for speaking of strange things, because of their very strangeness. Thus things can be said that one would be embarrassed to say in a normal fashion. Poetry, if it's not clothed in the strangeness of verse, looks presumptuous—like certain dances that have to be performed in masks or costume. I, too, have always thought that to express certain things I had to transform them into jokes, puns, or anyway into strangeness: so-called humor. To clothe reality so that it will be "forgiven." I realize I'm not explaining it very well, but this seems to me the true essence of humor. Forgiven by whom, then? By those who might think you presumptuous if you told them certain things in a direct way. You yourself have to be forgiven and accepted by yourself.

Reflections in water belong to this kind of poetic strangeness. It is a great joy for me to observe them, especially on hot days, when the light is perfect and the strangest symmetries are generated: two swans swim toward each other, with two other reflected swans, perhaps a heraldic insignia. Tropical islands, doubled ships, trains passing upside down over a bridge, the moon. Everything with perfect colors. If you look only at the reflection, and not at the reflecting part, you see a gratuitous reality that exists for you alone. For fun I throw a stone into the upside-down landscape, and seeing that the lower part moves I almost expect the upper part to move too. In the rearview mirror of the automobile I see a whole road, I see a sunset, the last little bit of sun disappearing behind the hills, and at the same time, in front of me, the reflection of this sunset in the eastern clouds, which is often more beautiful than the actual sunset, more elegant, less vulgar. In New York you may happen to see a sunset on the East Side, the sky there acting as a mirror to the sunset. The real sunset, coming from New Jersey, is uglier, as though the fact of coming from New Jersey made it in bad taste. The sky, or buildings, or fragments of architecture are reflected in puddles like scattered pieces of a puzzle. The reflection I see in a puddle continues in a glass of water that I hold in my hand.

In Romania, on moonlit nights, the peasant women used to look down into a well until they saw the reflection of the moon. Then they let down a pail, slowly drew up water with the moon in it and, with a spoon, drank its reflection. Looking down into the well at that moment, they could see the face of their future bridegroom.

———

One phenomenon that, although its nature is different, may have a place in the family of reflections is the shadow, the shadows that people carry with them, especially the long shadows of winter, which sometimes follow level lines but when passing over uneven terrain produce the effect of distorting mirrors. Then there's the shadow of someone standing at night in electric light on the sidewalk close to a wall—it starts at his feet, goes to the wall, and then continues vertically up the wall, just like a Mexican leaning against the wall and taking his siesta.

The cartoonist's profession is a difficult one, especially because you have to be your own editor: eliminate, eliminate, eliminate. A painting, a collage of pencils, a landscape—I do them with pleasure and ease. They are delights compared with the torture of finding an idea and then representing it in a less personal way, since otherwise you spoil the clarity of the idea. In the morning I set a notebook and pencil in front of me and start drawing. What should I do? What will I do? I feel lost, I seem to have no more ideas. But then it's not true; and the morning hours spent, for many years, trying to find an idea have preserved in me a kind of intellectual vigor that today I would no longer have if instead I had gone on doing what I know how to do very well—landscapes, watercolors. What is most difficult is to eliminate a lot of things rapidly. At other times the mind's computer must allow a vertical element to pass through all the horizontal possibilities. But above all I must be ready to combine ideas in the most unpredictable ways.

Once I've found the idea, or rather the vein, I feel, oddly enough, that the idea is not new to me. It's as though, digging in an archaeological site, I found something that was logically there and formed part, as a fragment, of something else I knew. I mean that what I've found is something that for the moment I'd merely forgotten. Sometimes you think you've understood everything and then you're amazed when, a few minutes later, you realize that you've understood nothing, you no longer remember what you had understood. You understand through an emotion. I felt truly happy when for the first time I understood that I understood. It's difficult to explain it: to understand that one has understood, to understand that the thing is possible, and that even if it's lost today, it's never lost forever.

never like to sell my work. I enjoy selling the rights of reproduction and keep most of my original drawings. I believe every artist would like to sell only the reproduction rights. Except for the ones who make giant paintings—they are very happy to get rid of them. And sculptors: there's nothing more tragic than the unsuccessful sculptor, faced constantly by his large, reproachful objects.*

The art world is so complex, amateurish, full of the unexpected, also because it's strictly bound up with

*Quoted from Robert Hughes, "The World of Steinberg," *Time*, April 17, 1978, p. 36. (Reprinted in Hughes, *Nothing If Not Critical*, Alfred A. Knopf, New York, 1990, pp. 264–65.)

fame and money. It is a special world that at times bears some resemblance to the world of pimps. The intermediaries transform into money the passion for art, of both those who produce it and those who buy it. Part of the poetry, the soul, the intelligence of a person gets bought (or sold). Here social and financial relations are more complicated and difficult. The friendship between the gallery owner and the painter is often like the one between the crocodile and the stork in Kipling's poem. Painting is a holy thing, which is for sale. Relics, bones of saints, are for sale. . . .

I have a small drawing by Klee on which, if you look closely, you can see a hair—from his mustache or eyebrow, it's hard to tell—embedded in the ink ever since it was liquid. And so I, too, have my relic: a hair of Klee.

Don't ever let yourself be photographed laughing or smiling, Barnett Newman once told me. If they want to take your picture, put on your best clothes, show your most pleasing expression but without smiling, a serious, even placid expression, because the dignity of the profession is at stake, the dignity of being a painter, an artist. Photographers want to make you look regular, normal, someone like everyone else, so as to be able to say: "What does he have that we don't have? Anyone can do what he does."

In architecture school someone (I don't remember who) gave me this useful advice: When you drop an eraser on the floor, don't rush to pick it up; watch it bounce and wobble until it stops, and only then go and get it. And likewise: When you have to screw the caps back on your paint tubes after using several in a hurry without closing them, never pick up the tube and go looking for the cap; take the cap and look for the tube. It's much easier.

I learned many things from Sig Lomaky, a very skilled Finnish carpenter. He made drawing tables for my studio, wooden panels, ladders. It was a great pleasure to watch him work. He fixed some wooden objects for me that had gone wrong: tables that I'd made myself, and which were crooked because they'd been improperly glued. He had clever tricks for correcting my mistakes, and the repaired tables looked better from the back, because of the reinforcements and corrections he'd made, than in front.

When he needed a piece of wood for some job, he chose it carefully, looked at it as though asking it who it was, examined its grain, and looked for suggestions from the wood itself. For me it was a lesson to be taken as a rule of life: never do things by chance, never exaggerate needlessly, as when one gives too much importance to a person, or too much love, or an excessive tip. To pick up something from the floor, he bent over with his back without bending his knees: he was a machine for picking up pieces of wood, nails, or what have you. When I asked him how much I owed him for his work, he was immediately embarrassed. For him these questions were torture, and he usually tried to work for a contractor, earning less but thus avoiding having to speak of money directly with his clients.

Physically he resembled those artists of the workman type, like Pollock, Franz Kline, de Kooning, and others, who know how to fix cars and are handy with tools, almost all of these guys foreigners or poor, and traditionally lacking in culture. People who all of a sudden, for some obscure reason, have become refined.

Like many of these artists, Lomaky had that touching expression of an unhappy child that one often sees on the faces of alcoholics, the sorrowful and at the same time seductive eyes of a child who has just stopped crying, of an orphan. Once in a while he came to the studio even without a specific job: it had seemed to him a good idea to come and see me, driven also by the courage he got from gin—I could tell by the way he walked. But outside of work our relations took on an unnatural character. The right way to talk with him was for both of us to work together and tell each other the things that every so often emerged spontaneously from whatever we were doing: things spoken without look-

ing at each other, both of us in profile, turned in opposite directions.

He came to see a show of mine. When he entered the
gallery and saw the objects on which he'd worked, he felt
ill at ease: these were things he didn't understand and
didn't want to accept. He had worked for theatrical set
designers; he knew how to make tables in perspective,
strange objects that, when he saw them finished and
functioning on the stage, he had no trouble understand-
ing. In this case, however, he had made objects whose
use he didn't really understand. If later he heard how
much money people paid for them, it only increased his
embarrassment. He felt he'd been made a fool of.

The last time he showed up it was to bring me a
present. Unfortunately, the present, which must have
cost him a lot of labor, belonged to that class of useless
oddities called gift items: an octagonal plywood box,
carved on the sides to show the different layers and colors of the wood, and with a lid very hard to make—a
piece of gratuitous acrobatics, a job by a boring specialist, a miserable effort to create an art object that in no

way reflected the talent, freedom, and pleasure that he usually put into his work. He wanted to call me "Professor": and thus I was no longer a friend, a colleague, someone to whom it would never have occurred to him to offer such a gift.

Between 1945 and 1992 Steinberg published ten volumes of drawings, and two books with drawings accompanied by texts by John Hollander and Ian Frazier. To these I add a number of catalogs, representing his more important exhibitions, and lists of the subjects treated in three of the volumes of drawings, lists written by Steinberg himself.

—A.B.

All in Line, Duell, Sloan & Pearce, New York, 1945.
The Art of Living, Harper & Brothers, New York, 1949.
The Passport, Harper & Brothers, New York, 1954.
    Subjects treated in this volume:
    False documents, passports, diplomas, certificates,
    false photographs (with false autographs), false etch-
    ings, false wine labels, letters, diaries, manuscripts,
    false ex-votos, calligraphy and cacography.
    Fingerprints, parades, cocktail parties, ballet, bil-
    liards, cowboys, [baseball] pitchers, palm trees, cats,

> dogwalkers, horsewomen, guitar players, automobiles, locomotives, railway stations, bridges, summer and winter, fashions, sphinxes.
>
> Victorian architecture, Art Nouveau, rubber-stamp architecture, slums, skyscrapers.
>
> Travel notes from Western Europe, Middle East, Middle West, Palm Beach, Istanbul, Manaus, and Hollywood.

Dessins, Gallimard, Paris, 1956.

The Labyrinth, Harper & Brothers, New York, 1960.
> Subjects treated in this volume:
>
> Illusion, talks, women, cats, dogs, birds, the cube, the crocodile, the museum, Moscow and Samarkand (winter 1956), other Eastern countries, America, motels, baseball, horse racing, bullfights, art, frozen music, words, geometry, heroes, harpies, etc.

The Catalogue, Meridian Books, World Publishing Company, Cleveland and New York, 1962.

La Masque, texts by Michel Butor and Harold Rosenberg, Maeght Editeur, Paris, 1966.

Derrière le Miroir, no. 157, Maeght Editeur, catalog of exhibition at the Galerie Maeght in Paris, 1966.

Derrière le Miroir, no. 192, catalog of exhibition at the Galerie Maeght in Paris, 1971, text by Jacques Dupin.

Derrière le Miroir, no. 205, catalog of exhibition at the Galerie Maeght in Paris, 1973.

The Inspector, Viking Press, New York, 1973.

   Subjects treated in this volume:

   Parades, biographies, masks, streets and avenues, time
   and space, music-writing, rubber-stamp architecture
   and society, the professional avant-garde, the law of
   gravity, urban war, cloud formations, words and letters, crocodiles, cowboys, girls, and diners.

*Steinberg at the Smithsonian—The Metamorphoses of an
   Emblem,* Preface by John Hollander, Smithsonian
   Institution Press, Washington, D.C., 1973.

Derrière le Miroir, no. 224, catalog of exhibition at the
   Galerie Maeght in Paris, 1977, text by Italo Calvino.

Saul Steinberg, edited by Harold Rosenberg, catalog of the
   retrospective exhibition at the Whitney Museum of
   American Art, Alfred A. Knopf in association with the
   Whitney Museum of American Art, New York,
   1978.

The Passport, revised and enlarged edition, Introduction by
   John Hollander, Vintage Books, New York, 1979.

Steinberg, catalog of exhibition at the Pace Gallery,
   New York, 1982, text by Italo Calvino.

Dal Vero, portraits by Saul Steinberg, text by John
   Hollander, Library Fellows of the Whitney Museum of
   American Art, New York, 1983.

Steinberg, catalog of exhibition at the Kunsthalle in
   Nuremberg, 1988, text by Italo Calvino.

Canal Street, Ian Frazier and Saul Steinberg, Library Fellows
of the Whitney Museum of American Art,
New York, 1990.

The Discovery of America, Introduction by Arthur C. Danto,
Alfred A. Knopf, New York, 1992.

SAUL STEINBERG was born in 1914 in the small Romanian town of Ramnicul-Sarat. Six months later the family—his mother, Rosa, his father, Moritz, and his older sister, Lica—moved to Bucharest. His father was a printer, bookbinder, and manufacturer of cardboard boxes. After high school, Steinberg attended the University of Bucharest for a year, studying philosophy and literature. In 1933, he went to Milan and remained for eight years, learning Italian and even some Milanese dialect, taking a degree in architecture, and drawing. Cartoons for the satirical magazine *Bertoldo* brought him his first fame. In 1941, after the imposition of the racial laws, he was able to get out of Italy, and eventually reached America by way of Santo Domingo. By 1943 he had become an American citizen. He served as a naval officer in World War II, stationed in China, India, and Italy. He married the painter Hedda Sterne in 1944. As an artist in New York he had immediate success, contributing to various magazines, in particular *The New Yorker*, and later exhibited all over the world. His publications were many and included ten books of drawings. Steinberg lived in New York City and in the town of Springs, Long Island, where this book was conceived. He died in 1999.

ALDO BUZZI was born in Como, in northern Italy, in 1910. He studied architecture in Milan with Steinberg, and there began a lifelong friendship. Like Steinberg, Buzzi profited by the study of architecture but did not become an architect. He worked first in the cinema, then for a publishing house. He began to write late in life. Two of his books have been published in the United States: *Journey to the Land of the Flies* (Random House, 1996, and Steerforth Italia, 1999), *The New York Times Book Review* Notable Book of the Year 1996, and *A Weakness for Almost Everything* (Steerforth Italia, 1999).

ABOUT THE TRANSLATOR

JOHN SHEPLEY's translation of Pier Pasolini's *Roman Nights and Other Stories* won the first Italo Calvino Translation Award, in 1987. He also translated Roberto Calasso's *The Forty-nine Steps*, which was published in 2001

The text of this book was set in Filosofia. It was designed in
1996 by Zuzana Licko, who created it for digital typesetting as
an interpretation of the sixteenth-century typeface Bodoni.
Filosofia, an example of Licko's unusual font designs, has classical proportions with a strong vertical feeling, softened by
rounded droplike serifs. She has designed many typefaces and
is the cofounder of *Emigre* magazine, where many of them first
appeared. Born in Bratislava, Czechoslovakia, Licko came to
the United States in 1968.